FUTURE FILES

SUPER HUMANS

A BEGINNER'S GUIDE TO BIONICS

Written by
SIMON BEECROFT
Illustrated by
STEPHEN SWEET &
STUART SQUIRES

COPPER BEECH BOOKS
BROOKFIELD, CONNECTICUT

© Aladdin Books Ltd 1998
© U.S. text 1998

Designed and produced by
Aladdin Books Ltd
28 Percy Street
London W1P 0LD

First published in the United States in 1998 by
Copper Beech Books,
an imprint of
The Millbrook Press
2 Old New Milford Road
Brookfield, Connecticut 06804

Editor
Jim Pipe

Design
David West
Children's Book Design

Designer
Flick Killerby

Picture Research
Brooks Krikler Research

Illustrators
Stephen Sweet, Ian Thompson, and
Stuart Squires — Simon Girling Associates

Printed in Belgium

Library of Congress Cataloging-in-Publication Data
Beecroft, Simon.
Superhumans : a beginner's guide to bionics /
by Simon Beecroft ; illustrated by Ian Thompson,
Stephen Sweet, and Stuart Squires.
p. cm.
Includes index.
Summary: Looks at possible future methods for
prolonging life, such as genetic engineering and the
use of artificial body parts. Also discusses robots,
artificial intelligence, cybernetics, cloning,
and other technologies.
ISBN 0-7613-0621-8 (lib. bdg.).
— ISBN 0-7613-0636-6 (pbk.).
1. Longevity—Juvenile literature. 2. Bionics—Juvenile
literature. 3. Genetic engineering—Juvenile literature.
[1. Longevity. 2. Bionics. 3. Genetic engineering.]
I. Thompson, Ian, 1964- ill. II. Sweet, Stephen,
1965- ill. III. Squires, Stuart, ill. VI. Title.
RA776.75.A54 1998   97-41602
610'.28—dc21   CIP AC
5 4 3 2 1

MISSION CONTROL

INTO THE FUTURE

Science is on the brink of such enormous discoveries that, in the future, the lives of human beings may be changed beyond all recognition.

Change on our planet happens faster all the time. It was about 4,350 million years before the earliest mammals appeared and another 240 million years before humanlike apes started using tools. But it took just five million years for modern humans to emerge. Since then, change has been at a dizzying pace: 8,000 years ago, humans learned to farm and to build houses; 400 years ago, the first scientific studies of the human body were published; 150 years ago, the Industrial Revolution transformed the world with mechanical technology, and just 40 years ago, the computer chip was invented.

Many scientific thinkers believe that the next big step for humankind will be the transforming of ourselves, our bodies, and minds, by new technology. The benefits are only just being realized. Artificial organs are now widely used, and computer chips are even being adapted for use in the body, for example, to improve a person's sight.

Research into our genes, the biological codes that are passed from parents to their children, is helping doctors to locate the genetic source of many diseases and to treat them.

In many cases, the theory of science is still beyond anything actually invented. Yet many scientists imagine a future that makes even the wildest ideas of science fiction look tame.

Many people greet this new science with excitement, others may fear it. But with this book, at least you can begin to prepare for it...

Right *Need to tell science fact from science fiction? Take a look at our Reality Check boxes. We can't see into the future, but these cunning devices tell us how realistic an idea is. The more green lights, the better. The "how soon?" line guesses when in the future the idea might become reality: Each green light is 50 years (so in the example here, it's 150 years in the future).*

REALITY CHECK

FEASIBLE TECHNOLOGY	○	○	○	○	○
SCIENCE IS SOUND	○	○	○	○	○
AFFORDABLE	○	○	○	○	○
HOW SOON?	○	○	○	○	○

COULD I LIVE FOREVER?

Many of us want to live forever. Maybe we'd also like to look beautiful, be super-brainy, or do impossible things like flying, breathing underwater, or running at 100 mph.

SCIENCE FICTION?

For thousands of years, people have imagined superheroes, like Hercules, performing amazing feats and living after death. More recently, science-fiction writers have also imagined what it would be like to live forever and whether the mind could exist outside the body. They have also dreamed up creatures, like Frankenstein's monster, that are made from human flesh and bone, and brought to life by scientists.

Today, science is finally catching up with fantasy. In the future, we may not be human beings, but superhuman beings. The exciting question is: Will the breakthrough come from genetics, computers, robotics, or some other science?

Above right *Science caught the popular imagination in the 1950s, a decade that saw the birth of the space age and major advances in genetics.*

Right *Ancient writers dreamed of a potion that made the drinker young forever. Today, some people try to hide the signs of aging using plastic surgery, but it can't reverse time.*

However, the same techniques can be used to rebuild faces disfigured by accidents or disease. New jaws can even be created using living bone.

Below right *Living forever was explored in Oscar Wilde's book* The Picture of Dorian Grey *(1890). In the story, Dorian stays young while a portrait of himself, which he keeps hidden away, ages and grows ugly for him. Dorian is selfish and lazy, though, and wastes away his time.*

Right *Many people claim to have had "out-of-body experiences," when they have the sensation of their spirit floating away from their body.*

Below *This four-year-old is Sonam Wangdu. He has been recognized by monks as the third reincarnation of a Tibetan spiritual leader whose last incarnation died in 1987. Reincarnation is the belief that after death people are reborn as different people or even animals. Buddhists believe in reincarnation.*

Main picture Many movies feature zombies — people who come back from the dead and who cannot be killed. But will science ever be able to achieve life after death?

LONG-LIFE HUMANS

Why do we grow old? The secret may lie in our genes. These chemicals, found in every cell, tell our bodies how to grow, how to work, and how to stay healthy. But certain genes stop working after a set number of years. If scientists can find out how to keep aged genes working, one day we may all live to 150 — or longer!

Right Genes are found on long, coiled threads called chromosomes. Shown here are the 23 pairs of chromosomes found in each human cell. In every pair, one chromosome comes from our father, the other from our mother.

GENETIC MIX-UP

In the 1986 movie, The Fly, a scientist uses a machine that can transport his body to a different place. When a fly accidentally gets caught in the machine, their genes are mixed up. The result is a creature that is half-human, half-fly (below). But today's scientists are a long way from mixing genes.

IT RUNS IN YOUR GENES

Cells are the tiny living blocks that make up our bodies. Inside each cell are genes, chemicals that tell the cell what to do. Genes contain codes passed on from your parents that determine the color of your hair and eyes, and even whether you will have sweaty feet!

The codes are created by just four chemicals inside genes, called A, C, G, & T (*page 9*).

GENE GENIES

Since 1988, scientists working on the worldwide Human Genome Project have been plotting the exact location of every gene — a bit like giving each one an address. Once they learn where a particular gene lives, doctors will know exactly where to go if it's damaged. One day we will even track down sweaty feet genes!

Inside a chromosome ——

LONGER, LONGER-LASTING GENES

The latest research studies the tips of genes. Over the lifetime of genes, the tips get shorter. Scientists have found that keeping the tips long appears to make genes live longer.

In experiments, drugs have been used to preserve the tips, extending the life of human cells by 30 percent — at least in a test tube.

GENOME PROJECT

FEASIBLE TECHNOLOGY	○	○	○	○
SCIENCE IS SOUND	○	○	○	○
AFFORDABLE	○	○	○	○
HOW SOON?	○	○	○	○

WRINKLE FREE

"Free radicals" are molecules that move around inside our cells, causing damage that can lead to wrinkles. Scientists believe that getting rid of free radicals would make us healthier when we get older. Some experts say we should eat plenty of fruit and vegetables, since these foods are rich in substances that may soak up free radicals and take them out of the body.

So, eating prunes may stop you from looking like one!

Free radical

The way the four parts of a gene combine forms a code that tells cells what to do.

—Protein

—Sugar

A STICKY PROBLEM

Many older people suffer from stiff joints that make it difficult for them to move easily. Only now, scientists are beginning to understand the cause. As cells get older, sugars in the body bind with proteins to form a sticky, weblike coating (*above*). Scientists are working on medicines that will "unstick" the gooey cells.

CLONE ZONE·
Creating identical copies with genes

A clone is a genetically identical copy of a person, created from a single individual. In most science fiction, clones are created by mad rulers to form armies of mindless warriors. Now, with the first-ever cloned sheep, named Dolly (*see below*), human cloning may be closer than ever.

A SPARE SELF

Some people believe that human cloning would allow us a second life. Your cloned copy would be like having a spare self, which could be used if anything happened to you. You'd watch your double grow up, telling the copy where you went wrong and how things could be done better.

Left Scientists have even cloned monkeys. With genes just one percent different from ours, they are the closest species to humans to have been cloned.

Below *Identical twins have exactly the same genes, and look the same, but may have very different natures. It's the same with clones, which would be created by allowing a cell to divide into smaller cells, each of which has the same genes as the original (center). But after they are born, clones will be affected by their experiences and the people they meet.*

So while clones in science fiction act like mindless robots, real doubles are likely to be different from each other and their one "parent."

SCIENTIFIC DOUBTS

Many countries have banned cloning experiments involving humans, mainly because so little is known about the long-term effects of changing a person's genes. It might make a person grow old too quickly or give them a disease as a child that only adults should get.

Below *Dolly the sheep is the first mammal cloned from an animal skin cell.*

A   B   C   D

CLONING DOLLY

Scientists took a skin cell from one sheep (A). This divided into identical copies of itself. One of these was joined (C) to the egg of another sheep (B), from which the chromosomes had been removed. This created an egg with the chromosomes of just one sheep (D), not two parents. The egg then grew into a lamb.

COMING BACK TO LIFE

The writer Michael Crichton has explored ways in which we could see real dinosaurs again. The movie *The Lost World* (1997, *below*) is about an island still inhabited by dinosaurs. In *Jurassic Park* (1993), scientists recreate living dinosaurs by cloning cells from preserved blood. Crichton's idea is that dinosaurs could be cloned from blood cells, which contain genes for the whole body. Damaged genes would be replaced with genes from living relatives of dinosaurs, such as lizards.

HUMAN CLONING					
FEASIBLE TECHNOLOGY	◯	◯	◯	◯	◯
SCIENCE IS SOUND	◯	◯	◯	◯	◯
AFFORDABLE	◯	◯	◯	◯	◯
HOW SOON?	◯	◯	◯	◯	◯

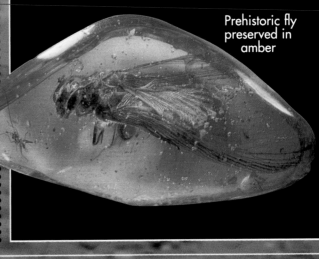

DEAD AS A DINO

Crichton's idea for cloning dinosaurs, using blood sucked by prehistoric flies, is unlikely to work. Scientists have now done tests on 30-million-year-old insects preserved in amber (below). They have found that only fragments of the insect genes have survived — let alone any prehistoric genes in the blood they may have fed on. Perhaps dinosaurs really are gone forever?

Prehistoric fly preserved in amber

MONSTERS OR MIRACLES?

Cloning could help couples who can not have children. Doctors would take genes from a cell in their body and transfer them to an egg cell to make a copy of the parents.

But many people are afraid that human cloning would create more problems than it solves. Would cloning become something that only the super-rich could afford, giving them the chance to see clones of themselves grow up as they grew old? Would dangerous leaders clone armies of especially brutal and obedient soldiers? Or would they clone themselves, over and over again, to form the ultimate army?

LIFE IN THE FREEZER

Could the key to living forever be found in a kind of high-tech deep-freezer? Some scientists believe that by freezing our body when we die, it could be preserved until science is able to bring us back to life.

There are already several companies offering just such a service — for the sum of $150,000.

COLD COMFORT

Cryogenics, as super-cold storage is called, has been used in sci-fi. Some writers imagine that astronauts who are traveling over huge distances in space can be put into "suspended animation." This means their heart, lungs, and other organs are slowed down, so that the body can keep going for hundreds of years. This is thought to be like being in a very deep sleep.

Left *Mr. Freeze, from the 1997 movie* Batman and Robin, *was created when a cryogenic experiment went wrong, and he was turned into an ice monster.*

FICTION BECOMES FACT

Now, cryogenic freezing has become a reality. Two U.S. companies, Trans Time Inc. and Alcor Life Foundation, are already freezing the bodies of wealthy people.

In this process, blood is first drained from the body and replaced with antifreeze. Then the body is placed in a tank, a sort of giant thermos flask. The tank contains liquid nitrogen, which keeps the body at a temperature of –326°F. In theory this should preserve the body for centuries to come.

Above *In 1991, a body was found in the Alps in Europe, buried under snow and ice — a body that turned out to be 5,300 years old. A Stone Age shepherd had fallen asleep — and never woken up! The ice had kept his body in amazingly good condition.*

FROZEN CELLS

These small colored tubes contain sperm and eggs in frozen (cryogenic) suspension. When restored to normal temperature, the sperm can be used to fertilize other eggs and the embryos will be allowed to grow into "test-tube" babies.

A HEAD START

In the movie Forever Young, *cryogenic suspension is a simple process* (right). *Real cryogenic freezing is performed far more quickly than ordinary freezing. This is to prevent sharp ice crystals from forming in the liquid around cells. These crystals would otherwise pierce and damage the cell. The frozen body is then kept in a special tank* (below). *Some people have had just their head preserved — as is said to be the case with filmmaker Walt Disney.*

CRYOGENICS					
FEASIBLE TECHNOLOGY	○	○	○	○	○
SCIENCE IS SOUND	○	○	○	○	○
AFFORDABLE	●	●	●	●	●
HOW SOON?	○	○	○	○	○

Many scientists think that cryogenics will never work. There would be too much damage to cells. But believers in cryogenics are *really* ambitious thinkers. They believe that microscopic machines (*see pages 14-15*) would get inside the cells and repair the damage.

Even if cryogenics really works, would scientists in the 22nd century obey your wishes and bring you back to life? Or would they experiment on you, steal your organs, or put you in a museum or a zoo? One of the scariest things is the brain — how much of your memory and personality would survive?

13

MICROMACHINES

Above *Miniaturized scientists battle their way through a patient's body in* Fantastic Voyage *(1966).*

Scientists are now developing micromachines that are so small they could travel through the body, repairing and rebuilding damaged parts — like sending in a team of microscopic doctors and surgeons.

TINY TOOLS

The new science of tiny machines is called nanotechnology, from "nanometer," meaning a billionth of a meter, about the length of ten atoms. It could mean that people never need to die, because worn-out body cells could be repaired again and again.

Below *These micromachines, consisting of cogs and levers, like tiny engines, are as small as a piece of plankton (a microscopic plant). Although they are tiny, they represent just the first steps toward even smaller machines that will be able to manipulate single atoms.*

ATOM BY ATOM

If these machines were small enough, they could even manipulate atoms — the basic building blocks of all things on Earth. In theory, one thing could be turned into another by switching around the atoms — waste, like apple cores, could be rebuilt into hamburgers!

To fit atoms together to create structures, scientists aim to use a machine called an "assembler." This would be like a mini robotic arm, operated by a new kind of computer.

GOING MICRO

The techniques used to carve tiny circuits onto silicon chips are now being used to make micromachines. Nanotechnologists are carving tiny cogs, levers, gears, and motors (right) *into silicon wafers.*

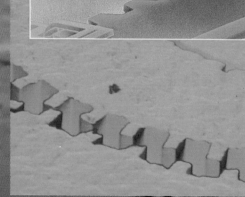

NANOMACHINES

FEASIBLE TECHNOLOGY	○	○	○	○	○
SCIENCE IS SOUND	○	○	○	○	○
AFFORDABLE	○	○	○	○	○
HOW SOON?	○	○	○	○	○

FUTURE SHOCK

Nanomachines could be used to search the body for disease (right). They would be able to reach the parts that surgeons' hands cannot reach — right into arteries and veins. But would people want tiny robots inside their bodies? What if they went wrong?

Another fear that some people have of robots that can manipulate atoms, is that they could escape from the laboratory and start evolving and building things in an out-of-control way.

CYBORGS · A terrifying combination of human and machine

They look human, they act human. Their skin appears real — yet underneath there's a layer of indestructible metal and a mass of machine parts. Science-fiction cyborgs are a terrifying combination of human and machine.

Right *The 1992 movie* Universal Soldier *highlights the danger of a cyborg that loses control.*

YOU *ARE* ONE
Cyborgs walk the streets today — you are probably one. Anyone who uses a telephone or wears glasses is a cyborg. This is because they are improving their natural abilities with mechanical and electrical add-ons. At the most simple level, this is what being a cyborg is.

HUMAN CYBORGS

FEASIBLE TECHNOLOGY	○ ○ ○ ○ ○
SCIENCE IS SOUND	○ ○ ○ ○ ○
AFFORDABLE	○ ○ ○ ○ ○
HOW SOON?	○ ○ ○ ○ ○

CYBORG IMPLANT

Artificial body parts (*below*) are increasingly common. Some parts are used by people who want to look more beautiful. Others are used to replace damaged or diseased organs.

Above *A silicon chip, inserted in the eye, can restore sight in some blind people. The chip detects light and passes electrical nerve signals back to the brain.*

Below *Artificial hands can be connected to nerves in the arm. Electrical signals are used to produce some of the movements of real hands.*

SUPER SIGHT
But now, more advanced attachments are being created, using new technology from a range of areas. Once again, science is catching up with science fiction.

A character in William Gibson's book *Virtual Light* can access different worlds with virtual reality (VR) glasses. VR headsets have now been developed to help the partially sighted access the real world.

BEST OF BOTH WORLDS?
Cyborgs are so powerful because they combine the brainpower of humans with the technological advantages of machines.

In Japan, for example, scientists are working on electronic muscles that will allow the user all the flexibility of human muscles, with much greater strength.

ROBOT COP

The combination of mechanical parts and human intelligence make cyborgs "superhuman." This threat is explored in science fiction.

The cyborg police officer in the movie Robocop (1987, right) is firmly on the side of good. However, Robocop 2 (1990) showed how dangerous it would be if cyborg technology fell into the hands of a criminal gang.

DIGITAL BRAINPOWER

Imagine how much time you could save, if you could learn a new skill, such as snowboarding or playing guitar, just by plugging a computer chip into your brain. The chip would do all the work of instruction books. Your brain would know what to do, even if your body had to catch up.

QUICK THINKING
In the future, plug-in chips might give you extra "RAM," to allow you to think at light-speed, or to improve your memory, perhaps for a test!

Below *In the movie* Johnny Mnemonic *(1995), Keanu Reeves' brain is fitted with a computer chip so it can be used as a "hard drive" for storing large amounts of information. The hero of the story is in trouble when he can't get rid of the information clogging up his brain. And what if it "crashes?"*

BRAIN CHIPS

FEASIBLE TECHNOLOGY	○	○	○	○	○
SCIENCE IS SOUND	○	○	○	○	○
AFFORDABLE	○	○	○	○	○
HOW SOON?	○	○	○	○	○

IBX-95842-QWY
90586x

HELLO, MR. CHIPS
If the brain could become a combination of biological and digital parts, it might be possible to store much of the memory on chips (*right*). Or perhaps our whole personality, including all of our memories and feelings, could be stored in a computer.

We would no longer have a body, but we would still think of ourselves as "alive" — even though we were stored in a computer. We could even be transferred from computer to computer across the internet!

Left *Fantasy often inspires real science, but sometimes gets it wrong. In* The Man With Two Brains *(1983, left) a brain is kept alive in a jar — which is funny, but unlikely.*

COMPUTER CONTROLLED

Neuromancer, written by William Gibson (*below*), imagines a frightening world of the future where people's minds are connected up to a vast computer system. In the story, it is very hard for people to escape the power of the system.

Gibson's vision of the future is not a happy one. He sees all kinds of problems created by technology having too much control over the minds of ordinary humans.

BRAIN FACTS

• The average brain weighs 3lbs — 2 percent of our body weight.

• There are more possible connections between neurons in the brain than there are atoms in the Universe.

• The brain is made of surprisingly ordinary chemical elements — carbon, hydrogen, oxygen, nitrogen, sulfur, and phosphorus.

BRAIN SPIES

Computers are already looking inside our heads to see what's going on.

PET scanners (*right*), for example, are used to spy on the working brain. They show doctors how substances, like sugar, are eaten up by brain cells, and which parts of the brain control senses like touch, taste, and smell.

BRAIN SURGERY

In the past, brain surgery was very primitive. Headaches and mental illness were treated by drilling into the skull. Electric shocks have also been used to treat people. Some people with mental illnesses had parts of their brain removed (called lobotomies).

New approaches to brain surgery include lasers (right), which are much more precise than a scalpel. Lasers produce less tissue scarring, so patients recover more quickly.

Doctors are also developing a new technique for finding damaged cells, using a semi-robotic arm that is linked to a computer with a 3-D image of the brain.

THINKING MACHINES

Computers can do many things brilliantly, but they cannot "think" for themselves. "Artificial intelligence" is the next goal for computer science: the creation of computers that can learn and teach themselves.

Above Chess-playing computers can beat human opponents — but they would not react if there was a fire.

FUZZY THOUGHT
Until now, computer chips have worked on a binary principle — they make simple yes/no decisions. The chips of the future will use what is called "fuzzy logic" to choose between "almost" or "nearly" right or wrong — like a human.

Below Neural networks are computer systems that "learn." Their circuitry is based on the connections made in the human brain. They have learned how to drive a truck by copying a human driver.

SURVIVAL OF THE FITTEST
Scientists also want to develop "genetic" software, which will be able to start from a few basic principles and learn as it goes. It would crash (destroy) any programs that are inefficient.

Right
Computer chips of the future may be specially prepared so that, instead of simply being programmed, they can "grow" like a living creature. Will we then have to start thinking of computers as living things?

LIVING CHIPS

FEASIBLE TECHNOLOGY	○	○	○	○	○
SCIENCE IS SOUND	○	○	○	○	○
AFFORDABLE	○	○	○	○	○
HOW SOON?	○	○	○	○	○

NEURAL NIGHTMARE?

Will computers one day be able to copy the workings of the human brain, with its vastly complex network of neurons passing messages to each other? If they could — would machines that think for themselves be in a position to take over the world, as many science-fiction writers have imagined?

Perhaps not, as computers would need to be connected to machines that could actually do things (such as missile launchers). Even then, we could simply pull out the plug.

Right In the 1968 movie 2001: A Space Odyssey, HAL is a thinking computer that begins to make its own decisions after receiving conflicting orders.
Today, experts are often surprised at the decisions that computers make, even though they know how they reached them.

LET'S TALK

The British computer pioneer, Alan Turing came up with a test for deciding whether a computer was "intelligent:" It would have to convince someone talking to it from another room that they were speaking to another human. So far, no machine has passed the test.

However, some scientists think we shouldn't build computers to think like us. They argue that the most powerful use for them is to create a partnership with human brains, so that two very different ways of thinking are working together.

This is an extension of how we work now. People think in different ways, so two brains can be better than one.

ROBOT REVOLUTION

Robots are already among us. They're used in factories to make cars (*left*), they're sent in to fight chemical fires, and they're an important part of the deep-sea submersibles that travel to depths too dangerous for a human crew. But these unthinking workers have always been programmed to do just one or two simple tasks — until now…

THE NEW GENERATION
A robot car has been built that thinks fast enough to drive within the speed limit. Robots are also being used by some police forces to arrest dangerous criminals.

Cleo, a robot doctor, works inside your intestines. Once the job is done, it crawls out of your bottom.

Right *The traditional idea of a robot, that looks like a metal human, is becoming less likely. Star Wars' C3P0 may remain purely science fiction.*

Above *We already have machines to do our laundry, but Woody Allen's movie* Sleeper *(1973), set in the future, has domestic robots that do all the household chores. Many experts believe robots could help the elderly and infirm enjoy active lives.*

FAMILY FRIENDS
If we are going to live happily with robots and allow them into our homes, we really need to be able to communicate with them.

The latest robots are taking the first steps toward recognizing people and even guessing our mood from our expressions.

They use T.V. cameras as eyes and sensors to tell them if any humans are standing nearby.

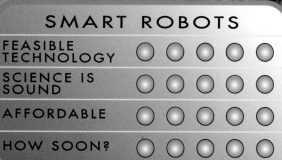

SMART ROBOTS

FEASIBLE TECHNOLOGY	●	●	●	●
SCIENCE IS SOUND	●	●	●	●
AFFORDABLE	○	●	●	●
HOW SOON?	○	●	●	●

Left *In the 1973 movie Westworld, a robot in a Wild West theme park starts to think for itself and becomes a killer.*

Such movies make some people worry about robots "taking over."

THE FIRST ROBOTS

The word "robot" was first used in 1921 by Czech writer Karel Capek. Capek imagined robots as human-shaped artificial slaves. For decades, this remained the idea of robots. Now, experts are going back to basics. Instead of trying to create fully-formed, pre-programmed robots, they are trying out much simpler machines that learn as they go along (*see* below).

ROBO-HELPERS

• **Robo pump** Germany now has the world's first gas-station robot. Two laser scanners work out your car's position, and guide the robot pump into position. Not a drop is spilled!

• **Cybermotion SR2** A robot watchdog, used in a museum in Los Angeles. It moves around with watchful sensors that can detect fires, gas leaks, and intruders. But it can't bite.

• **Robodoc** A robot that prepares the hole in human thigh bones before a hip replacement.

• **Victoria** A robot security guard, designed for warehouses. Some 6 ft tall, it has range-finding lasers that give it red pupils — just like the scary robot in the 1984 film, *Terminator*.

• **Dante** (*main picture*) A robot designed to climb inside volcanoes. It can withstand temperatures that would fry a human in seconds.

INSECT ROBOTS

The latest robots look more like insects than humans (above left). They are small, and stumble around like very simple animals. What is new is that they are not programmed to do anything except to seek light and feed on it. But they can learn from their mistakes. Such robots may one day be used in space exploration.

VIRTUAL REALITY. A new world without end

Like Alice stepping through the looking glass, virtual reality promises to allow us to inhabit whole new worlds that do not really exist, but look and feel as if they do (*left*).

VIRTUAL WORLDS

The aim of virtual reality (VR) is to create a believable 3-D computer-generated environment that users can move around in and interact with. A headset provides a view of the artificial world. The user's body movements are transferred to the computer using sensors in the headset and in a special pair of gloves.

Sci-fi movies, like *Lawnmower Man* (1992), give virtual reality a very futuristic look (*right*), but most VR is still very basic. Human figures are made up of blocks rather than having a smooth, natural-looking shape. This is because computers cannot yet draw and redraw the images fast enough to make a realistic world.

VIRTUAL CITY					
FEASIBLE TECHNOLOGY	○	○	○	○	○
SCIENCE IS SOUND	○	○	○	○	
AFFORDABLE	○	○	○	○	
HOW SOON?	○	○	○	○	

LIVING IN AN IMMATERIAL WORLD

Nevertheless, virtual reality is beginning to have an impact on today's world — and not just in computer games. Doctors can practice surgery on 3-D computer models, and soldiers can train on virtual battlefields.

At its most complex, VR could give people of the future a new kind of life. If we could store individual human personalities in computers (*see pages 18-19*), VR could give that person an entire virtual city to live in, with their own house, other people, and plenty of digital entertainments.

H O L O G R A M S

In science-fiction movies, people often live forever as holograms. Like Ben Kenobe in the movie The Empire Strikes Back *(1980), they can move, speak, and interact with those around them.*

Although holograms are realistic and three-dimensional (right), they are just pictures made by a special photographic process using laser beams. Unlike VR, which is computer-generated, holograms do not move.

Kyoto Date

"VACTORS"

Kyoto Date is the world's first computer-generated pop star (left). She sings and dances in her own videos, and is promoted as if she were real: She even has a "manager." There are already virtual actors, or "vactors." When the actor Brandon Lee died while filming The Crow, *a computer-generated stand-in was used to finish the movie. Technicians are now working on a virtual Marilyn Monroe, who died in 1962, but could soon be starring in a new movie!*

MUTANT BODIES?

The Sherpas are a people who live in the Himalayan mountains in Asia. Because they have lived at high altitudes for generations, their lungs have actually changed to help them cope in the thin air. What changes would happen to the human body if we were to live in other, stranger habitats?

Right *In zero-gravity conditions such as on space stations or on planets with low gravity, people would be able to fly or float around. Their body shapes would become less bulky.*

BREATHING UNDERWATER

It may be possible for humans to adapt to underwater life without using breathing equipment!

This could be achieved by altering the chemical composition of our blood so that it could hold on to oxygen for longer.

For example, crocodiles have developed blood that soaks up oxygen better, allowing them to stay underwater for over an hour. By mixing human and crocodile genes, perhaps we could create superhumans that can survive underwater.

SPACE FUTURES

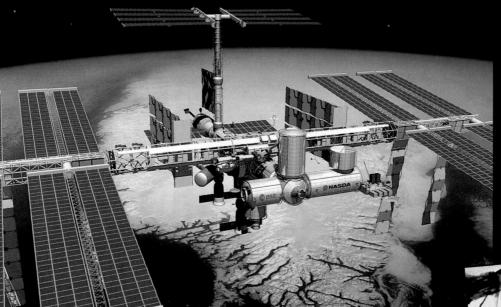

The International Space Station will be the first large-scale habitat in space. Many people think that it will not be long before the cost of going into space becomes increasingly affordable for individuals.

CYBORGS OR MOLES?

As the human population grows, many people believe that we will have to find new places to live. This could be underground, under the sea, or on other planets. Our bodies would then adapt to these different environments.

The first inhabitants of Mars might have to become cyborgs in order to survive its harsh climate. People living underground might develop eyes that could see better in low light.

Right *The movie* Waterworld *shows what might happen if the ice caps melted due to global warming, and the planet was flooded. People might adapt by growing gills.*

LIFE ON MARS

FEASIBLE TECHNOLOGY	○	○	○	○	○
SCIENCE IS SOUND	○	○	○	○	○
AFFORDABLE	○	○	○	○	○
HOW SOON?	○	○	○	○	

Gravely voices — because of the higher levels of carbon dioxide gas in the atmosphere

Larger lungs — to cope with less oxygen in the atmosphere

Stronger hearts — due to weaker gravity

Left *We might be able to live on Mars if we increased the oxygen in its atmosphere. After a few generations, Martian people might look like this.*

Bigger feet — to keep us on the ground in lighter gravity

27

CYBEREALITY •

Will technology really make our lives better?

What will it be like living in the future? Will we live in clean, robot-run cities that reach to the skies? Or, as we all live longer and better, will overpopulation create sprawling "techno-cities" that are hidden from the Sun by a thick cloud of smog?

Above *Tokyo, Japan, shows us what an overcrowded future city could look like. Its "capsule hotels" are built like giant honeycombs, with hundreds of tiny sleeping spaces instead of rooms. Each capsule has just a bed and a TV.*

HI-TECH OR LOW COMFORT

Many recent sci-fi stories see the future as a mixture of two worlds. In *Bladerunner* and *The Fifth Element* (*main picture*), people are surrounded by hi-tech equipment, but it only makes their lives more complicated. Imagine not being able to tell whether you are talking to a human being, a cyborg, or a humanlike robot.

Right *In the 1976 movie* Logan's Run, *set in the future, people live in an underground city that has an atmosphere that is controlled by computers.*

TECHNO-CITIES

FEASIBLE TECHNOLOGY	●	●	●	●	●
SCIENCE IS SOUND	●	●	●	●	●
AFFORDABLE	●	●	●	●	●
HOW SOON?	○	○	○	○	○

Flying squad: future police in the movie *The Fifth Element* (1996)

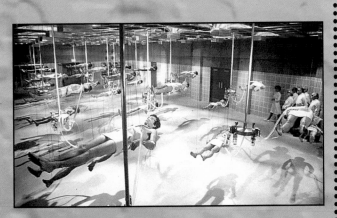

DIVIDING RICH AND POOR

Technology on its own will not make our lives better. Our environment is important too. Even today, cities are becoming places from which the rich move outward, to areas of light and space, while poorer people continue to live in crowded, rundown city centers. Science fiction can make us think about the potential dangers of letting technology run wild.

Left In the 1977 movie Coma, *people are kidnapped then kept in storage so that their organs can be used in transplants. Such movies show us that even new medicine can be very dangerous in the wrong hands.*

THE THOUGHT POLICE

In George Orwell's book *Nineteen Eighty-Four* (published in 1949 and made into a movie in 1984, *below right*), the future is grim. People are watched constantly by an all-powerful government, called Big Brother. There are hi-tech cameras everywhere and even Thought Police, who force people to live according to the rules.

Much of the technology in this book is amazing, but it should be our friend, not our enemy. Whatever our dreams, we're only human!

GLOSSARY

ARTIFICIAL INTELLIGENCE (AI)
The science of teaching machines to think like humans instead of simply carrying out programmed tasks or goals. The success of AI so far has been limited.

ATOMS
The basic building blocks of everything on Earth. Atoms join to each other in particular combinations to form different materials.

BINARY CODE
Widely-used computer operating system, in which information is represented as combinations of the numbers 0 and 1.

BIOLOGICAL
Anything that lives, like animals and plants.

CELLS
The fundamental units of living organisms, which, when grouped together, form tissues, such as muscle. In the human body different cells have different functions.

CHEMICAL ELEMENTS
The simplest substances, which cannot be broken down into anything other than themselves. Chemical elements include silicon, carbon, and gold.

CHROMOSOME
Structure within the nucleus of a cell, along which genes are found. Chromosomes occur in pairs in all cells except sex cells, which have only single chromosomes in their nucleus.

CLIMATE
The general weather and temperature conditions of an area.

CLONE
A genetically identical copy of an organism created from a single individual. The technique of cloning is relatively simple in plants, but much more complicated in animals. The first cloned animal was a frog, in 1952.

CRYOGENICS
The preservation of bodies by freezing them to a super-cool temperature at the point of death, so that, in the future, they can possibly be thawed and brought back to life.

CYBER
Refers to computers and machines that are controlled by computers.

CYBERSPACE
The computer-generated artificial world created by virtual reality systems.

CYBORG
An organism that is made of some human parts and some machine parts.

DEVELOP
Another word for evolve, which means to become more advanced. Species gradually alter through time and develop specialized characteristics that help them to adapt to their environment. Evolution has produced the millions of species that live on the Earth today.

DIGITAL
Computer system in which all information (such as pictures, sounds, and words) are converted into binary code (numbers) inside the computer, so it can be stored.

ELECTRONICS
Machines that are powered by electricity.

GENES
Segments of chromosomes that are responsible for people's characteristics, such as sex, height, and hair and eye color. Genes are passed from parent to child.

Every cell of an individual organism has an identical set of genes.

GENETIC ENGINEERING
Techniques that alter the genes or combinations of genes in an organism. By changing these genes, scientists can give the organism and its descendents different traits.

HARD DISK
A flat, circular object with a magnetic surface sealed permanently inside a computer. The hard disk can store large amounts of information as magnetic signals, similar to the way that sounds are recorded on magnetic tape.

HOLOGRAM
An apparently three-dimensional image produced on a photographic plate or film. The process was invented in 1947.

HUMAN GENOME PROJECT
Launched in the United States in 1985, this is an ongoing project to map all the genes in the human cell, in order to understand the function of each one.

INTERNET
A worldwide computer communications network. Anyone with a computer, a modem, and a telephone can be connected to the internet.

LASER
A device that produces a very strong, sharp beam of light.

LIGHT-SPEED
The speed at which light travels — 670 million miles per hour, or 187,370 miles per second. Nothing travels faster than light.

NANOTECHNOLOGY
The technology of making and using microscopic-sized machines, based on the word "nano," an abbreviation for a billionth.

NEURAL NET
A super-advanced computer system that imitates the complex way in which the human brain works.

NEURONS
Basic cells in the body that carry information to and from the brain.

NUCLEUS
The structure at the center of body cells that controls all the cell's activities.

PROTEINS
Substances that are needed for development and growth in plants and animals. They also carry out vital chemical functions.

RAM
Random Access Memory (or RAM) is the system that computers use to save information so it can be found again easily.

ROBOT
A machine that is programmed to do certain tasks and that, unlike a computer, can move.

SILICON CHIP
A wafer of the material silicon on which the pattern of an electronic circuit is scratched.

THREE-DIMENSIONAL (3-D)
The three dimensions of things that are solid — length, breadth, and width. In computers, it refers to how objects on a screen can be made to look 3-D.

TISSUE
A group of similar cells that do the same job, such as muscle.

VIRTUAL REALITY
A computer-generated imaginary world, used widely in computer games. Special gloves and glasses transmit movements of the user to the computer, which modifies the surroundings accordingly. This makes it possible to "touch" objects and "look" around.

INDEX

PHOTO CREDITS

Abbreviations: t-*top*, m-*middle*,
b-*bottom*, r-*right*, l-*left*, c-*center*.
Front cover, 24tr: 1st Independant
Allied Vision, Courtesy Kobal
Collection;1, 21b, 28tr, 29tl: MGM,
Courtesy Kobal Collection; 2, 10m,
11b, 12bl, 13b, 24b, 25 both, 26b,
28tl: Frank Spooner Pictures; 6tl:
Hulton Getty; 6tr: Kobal Collection;
6b, 7mr, 8tl, 10t, 10b, 20t: Rex
Features; 7b, 11m, 12t, 13t: Ronald
Grant Archive; 8b, 22b: 20th
Century Fox, Courtesy Kobal; 12br,
14bl, 14br, 16b, 18b, 19m, 20b,
21t, 23m: Science Photo Library;
16t, 18t: Tri-Star, Courtesy Kobal
Collection; 17: Orion, Courtesy
Kobal Collection; 19tl: Warner
Bros, Courtesy Kobal Collection;
19tr: Roger Vlitos; 22tl: Solution
Pictures; 22tr: United Artists,
Courtesy Kobal Collection; 23b,
24tl, 6m, 27: NASA; 29m: Virgin,
Courtesy Kobal Collection; 28-29b:
Columbia-Tri-Star, Courtesy Kobal
Collection.